THE MIND OVERLAY

Wake Up & Get Real.
A Guide to Transform Your Life

By Manuel Jose Muros

MANUEL JOSE MUROS

DEDICATION

To those who know the world needs change.

That change needs to come through us
as co-creators of reality.

Our children, our children's children, and generations to
come are dependent on the choices we make
and our willingness to do the work and wake up to
our divine potential for pure love and inner peace.

This is the change that changes everything.

ACKNOWLEDGEMENTS

It is with great gratitude that I want to recognize and give thanks to my generous friends and family who have supported me in bringing these words to life.

My dear friends Bill Hagen and Doreen Fay, who lovingly edited and guided me in how best to express my thoughts and teachings.

My dear friends Alan & Harriet Lewis and the Alnoba Foundation for believing in me and my teachings and their support in the creation of The Alnoba Peace Foundation.

I am delighted that Kurt Leland wrote the Foreward. He is someone that I appreciate and admire as a wisdom teacher and as a beautiful human being.

Once again, Mariella Travis has created a stunning cover to represent my book. Her creative talents and inner beauty shine in everything she does. Very grateful to have her as my daughter.

Words cannot really capture how instrumental my partner Alise Ashby is in all my creative projects. She is the wind beneath my wings directly overseeing all aspects of the creative process. Always present, full of love and wisdom.

TABLE OF CONTENTS

Dedication

Acknowledgments

Foreword ix

Introduction xi

The Mind Overlay 14

Cultivating Silence 18

Our North Star 25

    Desire

    Devotion

    Surrender

Our Responsibilities 32

    Attitude

    Alignment

    Action

The Art of Unknowing 38

You Are the Lead Actor in Your Life 42

Life is a Vibrational Game 44

Cycles of Our Lives 47

Well-Being - a Foundational Practice 50

Purification 52

Be an Energy Giver 58

Working With and Through Fear 62

Cultivating the Being State We Want to Have 65

Conclusion 68

The Practices 70

FOREWORD

by

Kurt Leland

Do not be deceived by the small size of this book and its bold claim to be a how-to manual for achieving liberation from our limitations so we may live more joyfully and abundantly. Manny Muros calls this conditioning the mind overlay, implying that our natural state is one of spiritual freedom to do, be, become what and who we truly are, a soul whose divine purpose is to discover what happiness is and show others the way to find it for themselves. But this natural freedom is gradually lost as we overlay it with ideas about what happiness is—something to be sought outside of us, not in freedom but in conformity with what family, peers, and the surrounding culture demand of us and what we demand of others and ourselves. Such demands and our inability to live up to our own and others' expectations create suffering and unhappiness. Go figure—we seek happiness and get the opposite. That's the mind overlay.

From his own spiritual awakening, seeking, practicing, and teaching, especially within the yoga tradition, Manny has distilled the essence of many spiritual teachings and practices that seek to liberate us from our family and cultural conditioning. This distillation is unique not only for its elegant concision but also for its simple, clear eloquence.

Manny's voice as a teacher is full of quiet, trustworthy authority. His phrasing of teachings that most of us have probably encountered in other spiritual and self-help books has a special, mantra-like quality that resonates with our own inmost voice, never commanding, always inviting to consider. His explanations of the mind overlay are insightful and easy to understand. But the core of Manny's book is the set of twelve practices for achieving liberation from the mind overlay. These practices are described in a deceptively simple series of steps. But they are designed to be open-ended, to lead to endless possible variations and a lifetime of pleasurable and revealing self-exploration of our essential nature as life, joy, freedom, and abundance.

INTRODUCTION

Twenty-five years ago, I had a profound spiritual awakening that allowed me to see and feel the energetic field that is our basic structure. In order to deepen and understand this experience, I immersed myself in yoga, wisdom teachings and practices. I spent two and a half years in meditation and contemplation practicing 12 to18 hours daily. Since that time, I have maintained a dedicated practice of yoga and meditation, as a full time student and teacher.

In my first book, The Other Side of Me: A Journey into the Mystical and the Gems Revealed, I shared my personal process of transformation. I also included 120 teachings/meditations to contemplate as a way of living from this deeper perspective.

I have written this book to offer direct practices and teachings that lead toward the path of awakening. My intention is to demystify the teachings without losing the magic of their transformative powers.

I will explain how our life experiences are often created by unconscious and unhealthy life patterns. When we free ourselves from these patterns, we can become conscious co-creators of a more vibrant and fulfilling life.

There is no easy path to awakening. We are all evolving in our own perfect way within our own unique path. The spiritual journey requires us to move in parallel paths that are mutually supportive. One part of the journey is the intellectual understanding of our own true nature and the second part is becoming our higher truth. We expand our awareness and we function from that higher understanding. It takes nuanced knowledge to both heal and then evolve, toward becoming the best version of ourselves.

From both my personal experiences and in-depth study of ancient insights, I hope to offer teachings and transformational practices to empower you to align to your life's purpose. This is a how to manual for evolving from fear to love, from lack to abundance and from surviving life to thriving as a unique expression of divine light.

As the teachings are nuanced, I invite you to re-read and contemplate as you begin the transformative practices. The tools remain the same, but your skill level for working with these tools will expand with practice. As you cultivate your skills your evolution will unfold.

The purpose of this book is to guide readers to become conscious and active participants in our own evolution. I encourage you to become excited about engaging with life with all of its ups and downs while being aware that every situation is a lesson in support of our growth, our inner evolution, not our outer success. In this process, we allow life to refine and mold us into our highest potential. We cultivate an active surrender to each moment to fully experience the life we have been gifted.

When the integration happens, the "new truth" becomes a part of our subconscious mind. It becomes a part of our default mechanism for the way we perceive and relate to our world, helping us "evolve" in an integrated and holistic way.

THE MIND OVERLAY

The mind overlay is a concept that came to me in meditation. It is the way the Universe organizes our individual life experiences. It is the key for our empowerment and evolution.

The mind overlay is the unique mental, emotional and energetic imprint from which we experience life. It is our personal world view, composed of both conscious and subconscious patterns, from which we filter and experience life.

Each one of us has a unique perspective which we place over the reality of each situation, of each moment. It is how we interpret and relate to life.

Past lives, childhood experiences, societal myths and norms, family dynamics and our own predispositions all come together to create a "filter" from which we project and interpret all of our experiences and relationships.

Our fears, sense of lack, limiting beliefs, self-worth, are all embedded in this overlay we place on reality. We have layered endless stories which distort and impede our ability to be that peaceful, loving, joy filled being that is our potential and birthright.

We are so enmeshed in these stories, that we assume they are true. It is like wearing pink colored sunglasses and forgetting you have them on. Over time you are convinced the world is pink and everywhere you look your perception is affirmed. You are lost in your own delusion. This is the human experience!

I have laid out a path toward freedom and liberation from the trappings of our mind's overlay.

These teachings and practices are designed to help us unweave the knots that are blocking our divine light from fully expressing itself. They assist us in becoming free to live our joys and passions in harmony and love.

The thoughts and emotions that constitute our mind overlay create a unique vibrational template which organizes the world we perceive, and the experiences available to us. We are always co-creating. The universe is always meeting us based on our vibrational template. If there is fear in our being, there will be fear in the reality we experience.

When we are following our dharma, our path, from a place of joy and fulfillment, we are in harmony with our divine plan and all of the universe conspires for the greater good. We can deliberately and consciously co-create a reality that is a reflection of our true potential, which will give us access to directly experience our own true nature.

First, we need to understand the yogic philosophy and the metaphysical science that supports that philosophy. Then, with practice, we begin to live the teachings and insights from this more refined level of awareness.

Through intellectual understanding and spiritual practice, we gently refine our mind overlay. We evolve from a place of fear to an awareness of our divine nature and the interconnectedness of all reality.

The story of Adam and Eve and the forbidden fruit in the Garden of Eden can be interpreted to describe how we began to create this mind overlay over creation. We began to reject reality as it is, creating a system of right and wrong to judge, and attempt to dominate the world as something separate from ourselves.

As we loosen the grip of our alienated identity and know ourselves as part of the consciousness that is creation, we move closer to living within the expanded mind of God. Fear dissolves into the peace and joy of being in the beauty and love of life.

CULTIVATING SILENCE

Cultivating silence is the foundation of our practice. In some way, most of the spiritual practices are in support of cultivating silence. This is an endless quest of moving into deeper levels of our own being, accessible only through the training of our mind to become still and observe each moment.

Rumi describes silence as "the language of God." This is a powerful statement to contemplate. We can say that silence is the absence of sound or, more accurately, the absence of noise. Silence is what is left when we quiet our mind. When we silence our inner dialogue, we open to the music, the vibration of creation as it lives in us and around us, emanating from the natural world.

The yogic and metaphysical teachings describe our need to bring our mental, emotional, physical and spiritual self together into one moment in time and space. By training the mind to be "present in the moment" we create unity within the self.

As humans we have the free will to be in harmony with nature or to be separate from nature. Our mental constructs create a false sense of separateness that is the foundation for all of the human suffering. This false sense of separation leads to many of our deepest psychological challenges as well as our destructive relationship with "Mother Earth."

We are a drop of water inside the ocean of consciousness. Our thoughts create the illusion of separation. Once we cultivate the silence within, we become aware that we are both the ocean and the drop, inseparable. Only our thoughts create the illusion of being separate.

Long before we can cultivate this "unity consciousness", there are many levels of awareness to harness and explore. All of these are experienced as we become more aware of our thought processes, and we look to understand and shape our thinking mind and the emotions it creates.

We Are Not Our Minds

Most of us see ourselves as mind, body and personality. In reality our mind, body and personality serve our spirit. They are not who we are but rather are the tools we use for living life. Your arm is not who you are any more than your thoughts are who you are. This shift in awareness is paramount for our evolution.

At the start of our spiritual meditation practices, we work to cultivate the witness mind or the "observer." As we begin to observe our thoughts and emotions, we begin to develop a better understanding of our inner dialogue. We all tend to have obsessive thoughts that pull us into a way of thinking and feeling. At first we want to become aware of these distractions and notice how much energy and control they have over our world. By recognizing their existence their hold on us starts to loosen. Through the practices shared in this book one is able to replace these limiting patterns with positive ones and change our relationship with reality.

Mindfulness Meditations

There are thousands of books on mindfulness meditation. I will share my short and direct version for your practice. Mindfulness meditation is a practice of deep listening and feeling with all of your senses. This requires you to cultivate the ability to concentrate and be immersed in what is occurring in every moment of time. You work to have a direct experience of each moment as you hold the mind back from interpreting or layering any thoughts over the experience.

The Mind Thinks and the Heart Feels

A powerful path for cultivating awareness of the present moment is to practice deepening the abilities of our senses. By fully focusing our mind on the experience of a particular sense organ one enters deeper levels of awareness. The mind can learn to rest as it feels each moment. It is easier to invite the mind into an experience as the observer than to ask the mind to be silent and stilled.

Practice 1 - Mindfulness Meditation

• Set a timer for 20 minutes. You can expand the time as you become comfortable with the practice.

•Take a comfortable seat and commit to holding stillness.

• Close your eyes and begin to feel your body seated.

• Start to feel the breath as it pulses within you.

• Invite/cultivate a relaxed state within you. Release the jaw, relax the muscles of your face.

• Concentrate your awareness on each of your senses. Notice the sounds of the room, the taste in your mouth, the odor of the room, the way your skin feels.

• When your mind wanders, simply bring it back to your breath and the sensations in your body.

Practice 2 - Mindfulness Meditation

• Place a strawberry, a raisin and a piece of dark chocolate on a plate.

• Close your eyes and be mindful to fully take in the experience.

• Bring the raisin to your nose and gently smell it.

• Place the raisin in your mouth and slowly move it

around without biting it.

• Gently and slowly begin to bite the raisin.

• Allow the raisin to dissolve in your mouth and feel the flavor linger gently.

• Once the palate feels clear, follow the same process with the strawberry and then the chocolate.

Practice 3 - Mindfulness Meditation

• Select three pieces of music from different genres that you enjoy - Pop, Classical, Jazz.

• Close your eyes and fully immerse yourself in following the dance of the different instruments and vocals.

• Notice how the music makes you feel.

• Where do you feel the music in your body?

Practice 4 - Mindfulness Meditation

• Fill the tub with hot water.

• Add scented bubble bath.

• Light the bathroom with candles.

• Soak in the tub and become fully present with the sensations of your body.

• Feel the breath as it pulses within you.

• Invite a relaxed state within you. Release the jaw,

relax the muscles of your face.

• Concentrate your awareness on each of your senses - Notice the sounds of the room, the taste of your mouth, the odor of the room, the way your skin feels.

• When your mind wanders, gently bring it back to the pulsating breath and the sensations in your body.

• Once you become fully present, use the exhale of your breath to release and relax into deeper levels of relaxation.

Become the observer of your own experience. Try not to be judgmental or harsh with yourself. This is a mirror into how busy and untrained our minds can be. It is the point where we begin to practice taking control of our own thoughts.

OUR NORTH STAR
DESIRE | DEVOTION | SURRENDER

To make genuine progress on the spiritual path, I have found that there are three qualities that are fundamental for our success.

1. Desire *"Tapas"* - A burning desire to discover / reveal the Truth of who we are. This desire will be needed to sustain the practices that lead to transformation. The desire to awaken must become our highest priority, not one of many things on our to do list. It is vital for each day to be guided by this priority.

This is why in many religions there is a requirement that monks devote their lives to their practices. I have learned that what you make a priority in your life, is what will blossom and what you nourish and give love and attention to will become the fruits of your life's journey.

Personally, I don't believe it is necessary, nor the best path, to turn your back on life to pursue your spiritual evolution. I believe that you can use your every life experience as the highest tool for your evolution.

The monk or renunciate is trying to minimize the distractions of life. However in doing so they are leaving out many important experiences for growth. It is definitely a more complex path to be a "house holder" and be fully devoted to your spiritual growth. It is a matter of having your priorities clear.

Every situation, relationship, experience becomes an invitation to get to know yourself better. It is an invitation to refine yourself and fully evolve into the best version you can be.

2. Devotion *"Bhakti"* - We need to believe that there is something greater than ourselves, a greater power or intelligence that creates and holds all of existence.

For many of us, religion has shaped our understanding of this creative force and has also created subconscious relationships to this force. In the yogic traditions as well as in many other wisdom teachings, this primal force cannot be fully understood by our intellect. It can only be felt and known in our hearts.

The power of devotion and prayer is considered the "grease" of our spiritual practice. Devotion holds the practice together in an easy flow through our desire to open and connect to the Divine within and without. Devotion allows us to live a life committed to a purpose higher than simply satisfying our human fears and desires. Our ego self comes into the service of a higher good and serves to elevate us.

Through meditation, prayer and devotion, we create and deepen our personal relationship to this unknown force. We learn to trust it and it helps us move beyond our basic fears.

3. Surrender *"Ishvara Pranidhana"*- Recognize that your knowledge is limited and allow for something new to be revealed.

Our mind only knows what it has experienced or has been told. We live our lives projecting our past into the future. Day after day we simply repeat patterns. We tend to expand only when we meet a "roadblock" and are forced to try something new.

Every truth is relative. It is based on past experience and understanding. To deepen our level of experience and wisdom, we must nurture the habit of questioning. Is there a better way to see a situation? Is there another way to move forward? Questioning opens us to "listening" which allows for the advent of divine guidance. Only by surrendering our mental constructs can we be open to listening to something new and potentially better.

My spiritual awakening came about through using these three practices. Life gave me challenges that my mind was not able to solve. Since I was a child I always knew that there was a force, a mystery that guided our lives. I wanted an intimate relationship with that force. In my family the force was called God. When things became unbearable, I prayed and surrendered to this unknowable force. I felt its presence within me and around me. I was not a yogi. I did not do spiritual practices to manipulate my energy. I prayed and surrendered which allowed me to experience a reality that was beyond my thinking mind. Having experienced this opening, I sought to continue to deepen my knowledge and experience, and that's what led me to a multitude of wisdom teachings and the path of Yoga.

Through my teaching experience I have found this openness characterizes the students that "get it" and have a breakthrough. The expanded yogic teachings become tools for refining our mind overlay and helping us along the path.

The buddha offers us a perfect example of the interconnected processes of desire, devotion and surrender. Once he realized the hardships inherent in life, he had a burning desire to transcend the human experience. He became a devout and dedicated yogi maintaining incredibly difficult practices of that time period. His practices were so intense that he came close to starving himself to death. Yet, despite his devotion to his practice, he was unable to arrive at the "enlightenment" he was so willfully trying to achieve. In total disappointment he sat under that Bodhi tree and as he was left with no more options to try he surrendered. This created the sacred opening to receive the gift of enlightenment.

This dance of effort and surrender allows us to navigate in our spiritual practice, because both are needed in equal measure. The effort is in the focusing. The surrender is in the allowing.

Practice 5 - Insight Meditation
- Set a timer for 20 minutes - You can expand the time as you become comfortable with the practice.
- Take a comfortable seat and commit to holding stillness.
- Close your eyes and begin to feel your body seated.
- Start to feel the breath as it pulses within you.
- Invite/cultivate a relaxed state within you Release the jaw, relax the muscles of your face.
- Concentrate your awareness on what your true feelings and beliefs are about God / The creative force that sustains the universe.
- Contemplate the great questions - Who am I? What is the purpose of life? Who/what is breathing me?
- Practice questioning. How do I know that? Move toward questioning your own automatic beliefs. Be open to the great mystery of life.

Practice 6 - Insight Meditation
- Set a timer for 20 minutes - You can expand the time as you become comfortable with the practice.
- Take a comfortable seat and commit to holding stillness.
- Close your eyes and begin to feel your body seated.
- Start to feel the breath as it pulses within you.

• Invite/cultivate a relaxed state within you - Release the jaw, relax the muscles of your face.

• Begin a devotional practice. Start to relate to something greater than you. Pray, have a conversation, feel open to the Divine that lives within you.

• Be in alignment with your own belief system both cultural and religious and be open to new awareness and a refinement within yourself.

The relationship that you cultivate with yourself and The Divine will be the ground from which all of your life will come to expression. There is no relationship more important. This is the only constant from the day you are born until the day you die. It is a relationship to cherish, nourish and delicately cultivate by giving it your time and attention on a daily basis.

These first three chapters offer the foundational teachings that will support your evolution. These practices are to be integrated into your daily life like brushing your teeth, bathing and eating. They are fundamental for emotional, mental and spiritual well-being.

OUR RESPONSIBILITY
ATTITUDE | ALIGNMENT | ACTION

A wise person learns to recognize what is under his control and what is not. The outer world is beyond our control, but how we relate to it is totally up to us. The only thing we can truly shape and master is our own being. Having cultivated the "observer" in us, we can be conscious about the way we are interpreting and relating to the life we are living.

Attitude - Are we arguing with our lives? Are we not accepting reality as it is, and wishing for things to be different? Do we prejudge circumstances with a negative interpretation even before the day begins? Can we accept a cloudy day, a rainy day and a sunny day with equal openness knowing that each day has its special gift for us. Do we see a glass with water as either half full or half empty? Can we see it as a glass with water with no further interpretation?

Our attitude is the mind state with which we meet

the world. It is our inner reality meeting the outer reality of life in each moment. Learning to shape our attitude is fundamental to our evolution and our well-being.

An attitude that accepts life as it is and sees challenges as opportunities for growth and exploration is in harmony with reality. Life is constantly in a state of flux and cultivating an attitude of openness and reflectivity is key to minimizing fear and the need for control.

Alignment - Alignment in life is being grounded and centered within oneself. We can observe this quality in great athletes who remain mentally focused and move with effortless grace. You can also feel alignment when someone speaks with the authority of experience and knowledge. It is about being authentically integrated in the self.

Many of the yogic physical practices are meant to teach us to move from the center of our bodies to cultivate and maintain balance and integration within oneself.

Cultivating physical and mental alignment allows us to feel complete and safe within. A busy and nervous mind makes us unstable. A weak or tight body limits our ability to move and express ourselves.

By optimally aligning our mind and body we also

create direct and open connections for our energetic body. Alignment cultivates a sense of being grounded that is also light and lifting. Picture the gymnast who seems to float through their routines.

Being in integrity is also a component of proper alignment. I use the word integrity in its definition of being whole, undivided. The beliefs, thoughts and actions are consistent and integrated.

Action - We learn to execute clean, clear, precise actions for the desired expression of ourselves. We choose to exert just the right amount of force and effort.

Alignment and integrity are something one embodies, something we cultivate to "be," as the place from where we want to engage with our world. Once we become aligned and integrated within, our actions are expressed with elegance and clarity. We are in harmony with reality and life flows with a rhythmic ease.

There is no timidity as we express our authentic self and step towards our heart's desires. By managing our inner being we become master sailors of our own ship. Able to harness the power of nature, we are capable of venturing out into the far reaches of our lives and safely move into greater expressions of our inborn potential.

Practice 7 - *Insight Meditation*
- Create a journal.
- Write down the top three things that your mind is concerned about.
- Are you able to directly control their outcome?
- What is your attitude? Glass half full, half empty, glass with water?
- Is there an opportunity to see the situation differenly?
- Explore the "inner story" from which you are meeting this reality. Can you modify your story?

Practice 8 - *Grounding*
- Create standing mountain pose.
- Place feet parallel and hips-width apart.
- Lift your toes and tone the muscles of your legs.
- Isometrically hug the midline with your legs.
- Bring the head of your arm bones up and towards your back, letting the bottom tip of your shoulder blades come together and rest. This will open your chest.
- Take your jawline back so that your face and heart are equally balanced.
- Draw your ribs in.
- Slowly lift and lower your arms with the rhythm of your

breath. As your arms are moving, keep drawing the arms into the shoulder socket.

• Practice holding all of the above actions simultaneously and notice how you feel.

• Try to be gentle with your actions, but do hold all of the actions as you explore this level of integrated movement. Do you feel more grounded? More centered? Stronger? More alive?

There is also an energetic centering and grounding that accompanies the mental and physical practices. This can be most easily experienced by simple breath exercises:

Practice 9 - Grounding

• Diaphragmatic or belly breathing. This practice can be done seated or standing and can be added to any of the above practices as a way of becoming both centered and grounded.

• Bring one of your hands just below the navel on your belly.

• As you inhale, bring the breath down to the belly and push your hand out with your breath first. Continue to inhale up into the chest to your capacity.

- As you exhale, empty the breath from the lower belly first until empty of breath.
- Repeat breathing with both the inhale and the exhale commencing from the lower part of your belly just below the navel.
- You can release your hand from the belly once you understand how to physically bring the breath to the lower belly.
- As you inhale, visualize the energy moving down to the pelvic floor and to your feet.
- As you exhale, visualize the energy gently rising to the crown of your head and beyond.

Diaphragmatic breathing is the most efficient way of calming our nervous system. It grounds and relaxes us in the most primal way. If one is prone to anxiety this practice can be difficult at first. If one is used to being anxious or tense as a normal default state, as the body begins to relax it can cause a false sense of feeling out of control. My suggestion is to do the practice in short increments becoming acquainted with feeling relaxed. Once you break through the initial reaction it will be a wonderful tool.

THE ART OF UNKNOWING

"Unknowing" is a very nuanced concept that is found in the more refined wisdom teachings. It is a very powerful tool for shaping our ego thinking into a more expansive and relaxed way in which to engage with life.

Let's begin by acknowledging we are limited in what we know. The mind, our intellect, knows facts. It knows the experiences of the past. It has a set of pre-judgements from which it filters all new experiences. It projects into the future what it knows from the past. Simply put, the mind can limit what we are able to perceive and keeps us contained in our beliefs without questioning their validity.

Usually, when we feel safe and comfortable about a situation it means that we are assuming the past will continue to roll out into the future. We rest "knowing" that based on its history the probability is high that tomorrow will have a similar outcome. We are happy to continue with the script we agreed upon.

Basically the part of the mind that "knows," is what creates and projects the mind overlay from which we interpret reality. We see things in a fixed way and assume that it will stay that way. This leaves out many potential outcomes and opportunities we may wish to explore.

Unknowing is connected to the contemplative practices where in a state of inquisitiveness we ponder the deeper questions. In this process we look to identify our stories and assumptions on any given situation. We must strip down the assumptions to the naked facts. Taking ourselves down to our most naked self, we can observe that we have created our personalities as if we were creating a role for an actor in a play.

Through active questioning we can acknowledge all of the projections and assumptions we place on ourselves and others, which block our ability to see ourselves and others as we truly are in any moment of time.

We can begin to understand that we live in a society with man made values and concepts that are mostly disconnected from the truth of the natural world. We learn that our values and beliefs are only abstractly related to our real needs.

We divide ourselves by nationalities even though the earth does not have countries carved onto its surface. We dress and behave in ways that make us feel like members of a sub-group. This creates a false sense of separation from others. We also accept external definitions of success and happiness which only leave us feeling empty and unsatisfied.

Simply because we believe something, does not make it true. We must deeply question our own beliefs. This questioning will open opportunities for a deeper truth to emerge. It is a gateway toward freedom from our most limited self -- from the prison we create around our own being.

The majority of our fears and misunderstandings are based on erroneous interpretations of other's actions and their intentions. Questioning our assumptions and asking for clarification will bring peace and harmony to ourselves and our relationships.

Repeat Practice 5 - Insight Meditation

• Set a timer for 20 minutes. You can expand the time as you become comfortable with the practice.

• Take a comfortable seat and commit to holding stillness.

• Close your eyes and begin to feel your body seated.

• Start to feel the breath as it pulses within you.

• Invite/cultivate a relaxed state within you. Release the jaw, relax the muscles of your face.

• Concentrate your awareness on what your true feelings and beliefs are about God — the creative force that sustains the universe.

• Contemplate the great questions - Who am I? What is the purpose of life? Who/what is breathing me?

• Practice questioning, how do I know that? Move toward questioning your own automatic beliefs and remain open to the great mystery of life.

YOU ARE THE LEAD ACTOR IN YOUR LIFE

By this time your practices have revealed to you how your mind is always creating an overlay of interpretation on the reality of each moment. These are the conscious and subconscious beliefs and thought patterns we have accumulated over the course of our lives. These beliefs govern our very existence. An unaware person will rarely challenge this perception of themselves.

Aware individuals view themselves as a blank canvas capable of becoming joy filled, fully loving and compassionate, in harmony with our world. We are our soul's potential. We are expressions of life in the manifested world and we can co-create the mind overlay that will determine how we observe and act in the world.

Having developed a meditation practice that allows us to connect to the witness within us, we are able to fully see the creations of our mind. We can notice how pliable our thinking can become. In time we come to trust the benevolence of the creative energy that sustains the world.

Now we can begin to work with the mind's overlay on reality. We can start choosing who "I am" in this game of life. We can program our minds to perceive our desired individual qualities. I am peaceful, I am loving, I am generous, I am kind, I am healthy, I am abundant, etc.

We work to embody and express those qualities through our actions, and to hold our focus on how we are choosing to show up in life. It is a demanding practice. It takes focused and sustained effort to cultivate another way of engaging with life.

Of utmost importance, we must be mindful we are working on our feeling state. We must only focus on what we are responsible for -- what is under our control. We pay attention to our attitude, we align ourselves to our soul's highest purpose, and our actions come from this place of integrity. We do not measure ourselves by the outer world's expectations. The fruits of our efforts will show up in unexpected ways and at the appropriate time. Trying to control the outcome will only set us back. We must love for loves' sake and nothing else. We must find joy in the freedom of simple existence.

LIFE IS A VIBRATIONAL GAME

Life is a vibrational game - Peace and love are the harmonious emotions, the harmonious vibrations.

Have you ever wondered how on a planet with eight billion humans, we find and relate to people with whom we have a connection. You can walk into a room full of strangers and you will feel an attraction to some people and be repelled by others. Our minds might find ways to justify these feelings, but in reality they are from our primal intuition, an inner knowing that guides us.

We are attracted to certain types of people and by similar situations which keep our experiences comfortably constant and predictable. We tend to receive what we expect from life. Even as people and situations change, the underlaying experience remains constant. It might be dating the same "wrong" person or experiencing similar conflicts in different jobs. Wherever you go, there you are, and life will always meet you where you are. It is a vibrational match.

The best way I have for understanding this is by the awareness that all of creation is composed of particles moving in a wavelike form. We are energetic beings with a vibrational fingerprint. Based on our emotions and beliefs, we hold an energetic field that resonates and interacts with the world at large.

Notice how when you have moved into a new stage in your life, some friends are no longer in alignment with you and you simply draw apart. New friends show up who are a better match with whom you have now become. By cultivating and holding an energetic field that has a positive outlook and that is peaceful and loving in its very nature, you can align to a world that reflects back those qualities for you to experience.

This does not mean that life will not bring challenges. It means that the challenges will be met from a place of peace and love by you and most of those traveling with you. The same situation can have a complete range of feelings based on how you show up to the experience that life is offering.

There is a complete interconnectedness between

the mind overlay, our vibrational template and the world we experience. The thoughts we have create the way we feel. The way we feel creates the vibrational field from which we interact with life. Our vibrational field is how life brings to us the experiences that will match us.

It is through this cycle that we become active co-creators, shaping our internal world and allowing the external world to meet us in the quality of life we choose to experience.

Recognize how our emotions determine the thoughts we have and how our thoughts also create our emotions. Thoughts and emotions play off each other. We use this play to maintain a life affirming vibrational state. Engaging in activities that make us happy will create a more positive stream of thoughts.

Here we see how important it is to honor and take care of ourselves. It is through a calm mind and a joyful spirit that we create the vibrational state that has us thriving in any activity we choose to engage in. The more calm and joyful we are, the greater our ability will be to be "present in the moment." We will be perceiving the true peace and beauty that life gifts us.

CYCLES OF OUR LIVES

Our lives run in cycles and seasons. We can be comfortable for years with the life we are living and then we begin to feel that something is not quite right and that something is lacking in us. We have run our course and it is time for a different expression of ourselves. These times of transition are both magical and anxiety provoking as we begin to let go of the old before we can see the full expression of the new. The mystery can be wonderful, frightening, or a bit of both!

Although the only constant in life is change, we often resist by trying to bring stability to the flow of life. Accepting this reality and learning to be comfortable with the mystery inherent in life is crucial for a peaceful and joy-filled life.

We learn to anchor within flow by deepening into the witness within us. Remaining calm in our thoughts and grounded in our own being we hold steady to the qualities we want to embody as life dances with us. We learn to be led by the magical mystery of life. Similar to the female tango dancer being lead by her partner, we focus on our attitude and maintain inner alignment as we move through life's experiences.

For a new chapter to begin, another must end. Endings and beginnings are interconnected in the flow of life. By placing ourselves in service to a higher calling, we can give dramatic meaning to our lives. We place our lives in perspective when we recognize our part in the quilt of life. Accepting impermanence as a constant allows us to truly value change as a recurring gift in our lives.

Every season has its gifts and challenges. We start free and playful as children and as we take on society's stories, patterns and responsibilities, life begins to weigh on us. In the first half of our lives we are usually looking outside ourselves to become a valued member of society. We have the need to make something of ourselves. We look to be successful in the context of the artificial society we have created. Money, prestige and status tend to define how we see ourselves and others.

Whether we have become "successful" or not, during these cycles of our lives, we tend to assess how we are doing. We tend to start questioning what we have valued and who we have become, chasing those outer accomplishments. At whatever age you start asking these questions, know that you are at a fork in the road and that there is a doorway to a better life waiting for you. You can choose to live a life that is created from the inside out and measured by the quality of the person you are becoming.

WELL-BEING
A FOUNDATIONAL
PRACTICE

We have been given these magnificent vessels for our life's journey. These amazing bubbles of biology are capable of amazing feats and unimaginable experiences. Our bodies have the capacity to climb mountains, swim in water, run marathons and delight us with the pleasures of our senses. Our minds have endless imaginations, can understand abstract subjects, create incredible emotions and give meaning and purpose to our lives. Our bodies even have built in mechanisms for self-healing!

Our souls are explorers within this body. We are not meant to be in a safe harbor. We are meant to venture out and savor all the riches of our human experience. In order to successfully accomplish this we must properly care for our minds and bodies. The toxins of life corrode our vessels. Stress, unhealthy foods, toxic relationships, lack of exercise, and absence of spiritual practices that calm and center our minds and give purpose to our lives.

Our first priority is to maintain well-being by the choices we make on a daily basis. A strong healthy body and a calm clear mind are the ground from which we want to meet each day. They don't happen by coincidence. It takes effort and dedication to cultivate and maintain a healthy life. By taking care of ourselves we also become self-sufficient. We are doing what needs to be done to be healthy and happy within ourselves.

By taking care of your basic needs first, you are then available for others and for the challenges and gifts life will bring you along the way.

PURIFICATION

To achieve well-being, we must understand the process of digesting life and purifying our minds and bodies from the toxins of living life.

Monks will withdraw from life, minimize complex relationships, spend many hours in meditation / contemplation and observe a minimalistic diet as a way of maintaining purity in their lives. For me, this is very similar to having a beautiful sailing vessel to explore the four corners of the world and decide to dry dock it to keep it pristine.

Life is for living and it is important to be thoughtful and aware of how we engage with life. All aspects of ourselves must be properly cared for to remain healthy.

Every day we put our minds and bodies through a whole set of experiences. We eat different kinds of food. Some are easy to digest and generate quick energy, others take much more effort to break down and discard. Some of our drinks (coffee) are stimulants others are depressants (alcohol) which have effects on our nervous system.

Diets that are heavy in dairy products will create mucus and congestion in our nasal cavities. Everything we eat has to be digested by our bodies and what we eat has an effect on how we feel, the quality of the energy generated, and the effect of the left over toxins to be eliminated from the body.

The classic American diet consisting of meat, heavy starches and dairy products is fairly difficult for our bodies to digest in comparison to a diet mostly of "live foods" like fruits, nuts, grains and vegetables. This can be felt in the energy level one experiences, lack of nasal congestion and in the regularization of our bowel movements.

What we eat makes a huge difference in our general health and in our feeling state. The processed food industry has been addicting us to greater levels of sugar in our diets which give us empty calories and leads to craving those same foods which are neither nourishing or healthy.

On a daily basis there is also the quality of the air we breath, the water we drink and the ambient level of background noise. They all tax our senses and we have to balance and compensate for their wear and tear on us. It is important to detox ourselves from the constant bombardment of modern life by spending time in nature, controlling the amount of digital input we take in and expanding our leisure time with good quality human interactions.

As humans we are here to grow and evolve. This is accomplished by the experiences we have. Some will be be challenging, others sweet and enjoyable. How we relate to our experiences will be paramount in determining how well we digest our lessons and maintain mental and emotional equanimity which is key to our wellbeing.

The greater growth usually comes from working through challenging situations which will help us develop a new, more refined way of relating to those challenging situations. Life will polish us as a carpenter shapes wood or a sculptor carves the stones.

If we don't fully embrace the challenges that are in our lives or if we try to postpone them or ignore them, they will remain undigested in our energetic, physical and emotional bodies. They will show up as low back, neck or shoulder pain. They will create stress and anger in our emotional body. They will lead to unhealthy patterns of self medicating with drugs and alcohol or overeating. We are a complex system of many interrelated parts. Having a holistic approach to life is what will allow us to evolve while efficiently processing all that we need to digest on a daily basis.

When employing the many practices I have shared in this book, our goal is to achieve an inner sense of safety and embodiment. We must cultivate a calm mind with an objective perspective that can make life affirming choices with a clear and realistic understanding of the the challenges faced in daily living.

When you are confident in yourself and feel safe and secure no matter what the outcome of any situation, you will be able to fully engage in the process at hand, learn what you need to learn, and flow with what life is offering you. You will be healthily digesting life and fully eliminating the toxins left behind.

Mental and emotional "food" is digested just like physical food. We need to choose healthy relationships and a life affirming lifestyle while maintaining practices that will support our "vessel" for this life journey.

Practice 10 - Purification

• Food Cleanse - For three days try a diet that consists of just "live foods" - Fruits, vegetables, salads, nuts - no animal products including dairy. Eliminate or greatly diminish caffeinated drinks.

• Speech Fast- For three days practice holding silence throughout your day (eat in silence, go inward, request from household members a morning/evening of silence. It does not have to be three days of total silence, just work on creating pockets of silence.

• Input Cleanse- For three days eliminate electronic input other than necessary for work. No TV, No Radio (in car also), No Social Platforms like FB, Twitter, etc.

• Spend time in nature. Take silent walks in the woods, at the beach. Open all of your senses and feel the harmony inherent in the natural world.

• Have a positive attitude about bringing life affirming changes into your daily experience.

• Expand these practices to a five day cycle.

Use these exercises as tools for becoming aware of the relationship we have to all of these "habits". Try not to judge but choose to be aware of how they are impacting your life. Start implementing these healthier life choices into your daily life. It is helpful not to focus on what you are giving up but instead look at what your are adding.

BE AN ENERGY GIVER

A wonderful way to measure how healthy we are in our relationships is to see if we are needy or generous in our interactions. Through the practices shared in the early chapters, we develop the sensitivity to recognize if we are insecure, needy, afraid or timid with certain people or in particular situations.

We want to cultivate a state of being that feels safe and stable in who we are and not based on any external expectations. Life will change and we will continue to grow and blossom if we remain steady from within.

There is a tendency to assume that we are dependent on outer forces for what we have. For example, I have abundance due to my job or I have love because of a particular person. The truth is that because you carry abundance and love within you, the job became a conduit of your abundance and that person came to share in your love.

If one feels dependent on anything or anyone,

that relationship will be unbalanced and unhealthy. We want to carry the energy of appreciation and gratitude for all the blessings in our lives and also know deep inside that we are sustained by a force that will always bring our way all that our soul needs, desires and is able to receive.

It is very important to feel the inherent freedom within and to know that it is with freedom in our heart that we choose to engage in all relationships. This way, every day, we show up with peace and generosity.

I do want to clarify that it is quite healthy to feel the loss of a loved one and suffer a period of mourning when something or someone we value is no longer with us.

Practice 11 - Reframing The Mind's Overlay

• Take a comfortable seat and commit to holding stillness.

• Close your eyes and begin to feel your body seated.

• Start to feel the breath as it pulses within you.

• Invite/cultivate a relaxed state within you. Release the jaw, relax the muscles of your face.

• Take a moment to recognize those individuals in your life who seem to tire you out and pull energy from you. It is their sense of lack, translated into need that places un due stress in your interactions with them.

• Now, scan your mind for people or situations where you may be feeling needy, scared and somehow wanting to control the situation, not to "upset the apple cart."

• Take a few minutes in meditation/contemplation to feel how your subconscious beliefs and fears might be impacting your emotions and behavior. Question/ challenge your own thoughts and beliefs. Separate the facts from your interpretations.

(An example I use in my teachings is that when we are all sitting in the meditation room it is a "fact" -- we are all sitting in a room. Some may see it as a small or large room, a beautiful room, etc. These are the interpretations we place on reality. We can all agree to the fact that we are sitting in a room).

• Create a mental story where you can see yourself with love and peace stepping away from that situation/relationship knowing that all will be fine. Use affirmations - I am safe, I am loved, I am abundant….to create the feeling state that those qualities belong to you and are not dependent on anyone else.

• Having created an internal vision of your own security and worthiness you can then reframe how you can inter act in that situation from an energy neutral position. No one is needy. Your interactions come from generosity and a desire to give and share. You are letting go of the need to control the outcome allowing for its highest expression.

In this world of flow, everything has a beginning, a middle and an end. The world is not random. There is purpose and divine timing to our lives. Cultivating the ability to meet each day with gratitude and to share our gifts and essence freely creates a beautiful harmony with the flow of life.

WORKING WITH
&
THROUGH FEAR

I like to think of fear as the lack of feeling safe. Fear arises when our safety or security seems threatened. Fear is a safety mechanism that calls us into action to protect our physical being, our loved ones and our possessions. It can trigger a biochemical response of fight or flight in order to protect ourselves.

In our modern societies we can have complex fears that lie just below the surface. Many people live paycheck to paycheck with outstanding debt accruing high interest charges. Others have chronic medical issues with high prescription costs. Some people have uncertainty around their jobs or housing. Others are fearful of retirement and how they will sustain themselves.

To make matters worse, we are part of a consumer oriented society that is constantly promoting things and expensive lifestyles as the royal road to happiness and success. This outward focus makes it more difficult to sustain self-acceptance and self-love.

In a society that revolves around money and that is transaction oriented one can feel disconnected. This creates a deep rooted fear within everyday life. Fear over a sustained period of time will lead to anxiety and the inability to relax deeply. Fear negatively impacts our adrenal system adding to our symptoms of chronic stress.

For psychological and spiritual well-being we need to cultivate a sense of safety, a feeling of belonging, a sense of purpose for our life and a genuine self-acceptance and love of our own unique self. Unfortunately, I don't see a quick fix for contemporary problems. Our values and everyday activities are so far from the rhythms of the natural world and what is needed for societal healing. Consequently, all of us must see beyond the societal myths and stories and cultivate a more authentic connection to our true nature.

We need an antidote for the insanity of our modern world. That antidote can be found in the wisdom teachings that cross all cultures. It is by cultivating the ability to see our cultural and personal overlays over reality that we can start moving out of the insane currents of modern life and become an independent authentic being.

We must develop a sober honesty with ourselves and truly become naked with all aspects of self-judgment. Only from this rock bottom assessment will we be ready to surrender to the "unknowing" and its transformational powers.

Fortunately for us, the daily practices are not related to the shifting sands because their job is to take us "home." We need to cultivate silence, develop present moment awareness and maintain physical and mental well-being. The change occurs within us and it trickles out into all aspects of our lives.

As our false sense of separateness diminishes, we are able to feel and know the life force that sustains and connects us all. We can fully recognize that our true gift is our uniqueness. We can relax into the energetic loving embrace of our creator and be fully aware that we are a part of the divine tapestry.

Becoming safe and complete within ourselves allows our whole being to relax. It allows our minds to slow down so we can fully begin to see and feel the love and beauty that surrounds us. All of this is available to us through learning to align our mind to Absolute Truth and its ageless wisdom.

CULTIVATING
THE BEING STATE
WE WANT TO HAVE

There are endless ways we block our divine essence. Fear of material loss and the absence of self-acceptance and self-love are key examples. Our practice allows us to see the inner dialogue of beliefs that are shaping our reality, beliefs that keep us stuck in multiple ways.

How do we get unstuck? We begin to cultivate its opposite, the quality we actually want to experience and embody. This process can be used to change any behavior or belief in a gradual, non challenging way.

Everything in this realm is on a gradient. It is not binary with an on and off switch. So we just start moving from one end of the spectrum to the other slowly learning how to feel the way we want to be.

For example, H_2O can be experienced as ice, water, steam and it can move within those levels quite gradually. The difference is how fast the molecules are moving which is determined by their temperature.

Let's say you would like to have a healthier diet. Start by adding foods you would like to bring into your diet. It is best not to focus on what you will "need to give up." Focus on what you want to add. Move in the direction of what you want more of in your life.

This applies to any change we want to make in our lives. Move slowly into the feeling and actions of that way of being. If you would like to be more active, begin by taking a daily walk and get into the feeling and routine of what you do want to be experiencing. Every journey begins with one step pointed in the direction we want to go.

If you are looking to have more abundance in your life, create space between what you are earning and what you are spending. Any amount of extra money will create a sense of abundance. Spending money to acquire material things only creates a momentary satisfaction that is quickly eroded by a greater sense of need. If you have some money saved, you will have the "potential" of purchasing many things. You have created a feeling state of being able to choose how to spend the extra money.

You are now feeling abundance! You might even decide to keep expanding your savings because it feels so good.

Practice 12 - Reframing The Mind's Overlay

• Take a comfortable seat and commit to holding stillness.

• Close your eyes and begin to feel your body seated.

• Start to feel the breath as it pulses within you.

• Invite/cultivate a relaxed state within you - Release the jaw, relax the muscles of your face.

• Identify an aspect of yourself that is limiting you and that you would like to change.

• Identify its opposite, the quality that you would like to cultivate in yourself.

• Identify in which situations you already can feel this quality and deeply explore it while in this contemplative space. Really taste it and get intimate with it.

• Imagine/project the way you feel into other situations where in the past that has not been the case and see yourself embodying this quality you are cultivating.

• After having created this state within yourself, you are in a good place to try it out in real life. Take small steps in real life in the direction you want to develop in yourself.

• Focus on the quality you are developing in yourself and not on what has been challenging you.

CONCLUSION

All the teachings and practices in this little book are to help us become more aware of our true nature. We are on a lifelong journey of growth and evolution. Approaching life from this perspective aligns us to our true purpose.

All of the exercises I have shared with you are timeless with minor accommodations to the issues of our modern society. These are the tools that have been used for ages by wise men, sages and saints. They are meant to reveal your divine self. Once that has occurred, your inner teacher will lead you on your unique path.

It is by embodying these teachings that we become free of our "false fears" and the sense of lack and separation that is the foundational "dis-ease" of human conditioning. These practices will lead us into ever deeper levels of knowledge and insights. It is a journey with no final destination, as we are ever evolving on our way back to becoming our true nature. This inner world is revealed through dedicated practice. It is a complete shift of one's paradigm. My words can only serve as an invitation to explore all that is available within you.

The goal is to have a relaxed and receptive state as our default setting. From this point we have access to the "present moment" and we will experience the real beauty and joy inherent in life.

It is with great love that I humbly invite you to join the legends of humankind doing the inner work to become free from the trappings of our human conditioning. We are once again at a crossroads in our shared evolution and the choices we make will determine the future for generations to come. Let's anchor the energies of love and peace into our everyday experiences!!!

PRACTICES

Wake up to yourself. Wake up to the world.

Be free to be you. Be free to follow your heart's calling.

Let's get real… The world needs you!

Mindfulness Practices

Practice 1

• Set a timer for 20 minutes. You can expand the time as you become comfortable with the practice.

• Take a comfortable seat and commit to holding stillness.

• Close your eyes and begin to feel your body seated.

• Start to feel the breath as it pulses within you.

• Invite/cultivate a relaxed state within you. Release the jaw, relax the muscles of your face.

• Concentrate your awareness on each of your senses. Notice the sounds of the room, the taste in your mouth, the odor of the room, the way your skin feels.

• When your mind wanders, simply bring it back to your breath and the sensations in your body.

Practice 2

• Place a strawberry, a raisin and a piece of dark chocolate on a plate.

• Close your eyes and be mindful to fully take in the experience.

• Bring the raisin to your nose and gently smell it.

• Place the raisin in your mouth and slowly move it around without biting it.

• Gently and slowly begin to bite the raisin.

• Allow the raisin to dissolve in your mouth and feel the flavor linger gently.

• Once the palate feels clear, follow the same process with the strawberry and then the chocolate.

Practice 3

• Select three pieces of music from different genres that you enjoy - Pop, Classical, Jazz.

• Close your eyes and fully immerse yourself in following the dance of the different instruments and vocals.

• Notice how the music makes you feel.

• Where do you feel the music in your body?

Practice 4

- Fill the tub with hot water.
- Add scented bubble bath.
- Light the bathroom with candles.
- Soak in the tub and become fully present with the sensations of your body.
- Feel the breath as it pulses within you.
- Invite a relaxed state within you. Release the jaw, relax the muscles of your face.
- Concentrate your awareness on each of your senses - Notice the sounds of the room, the taste of your mouth, the odor of the room, the way your skin feels.
- When your mind wanders, gently bring it back to the pulsating breath and the sensations in your body.
- Once you become fully present, use the exhale of your breath to release and relax into deeper levels of relaxations.

Become the observer of your own experience. Try not to be judgmental or harsh with yourself. This is a mirror into how busy and untrained our minds can be. It is the point were we begin to practice taking control over our own thoughts.

Insight Practices

Practice 5

• Set a timer for 20 minutes - You can expand the time as you become comfortable with the practice.

• Take a comfortable seat and commit to holding stillness.

• Close your eyes and begin to feel your body seated.

• Start to feel the breath as it pulses within you.

•Invite/ cultivate a relaxed state within you - Release the jaw, relax the muscles of your face.

• Concentrate your awareness on what your true feelings and beliefs are about God / The creative force that sustains the universe.

• Contemplate the great questions - Who am I? What is the purpose of life? Who/what is breathing me?

• Practice questioning. How do I know that? Move toward questioning your own automatic beliefs. Be open to the great mystery of life.

Practice 6

• Set a timer for 20 minutes - You can expand the time as you become comfortable with the practice.

• Take a comfortable seat and commit to holding stillness.

• Close your eyes and begin to feel your body seated.

• Start to feel the breath as it pulses within you.

• Invite/cultivate a relaxed state within you - Release the jaw, relax the muscles of your face.

• Begin a devotional practice. Start to relate to something greater than you. Pray, have a conversation, feel open to the Divine that lives within you.

• Be in alignment with your own belief system both cultural and religious and be open to new awareness and a refinement within yourself.

Practice 7

• Create a journal.

• Write down the top three things that your mind is concerned about.

• Are you able to directly control their outcome?

• What is your attitude? Glass half full, half empty, glass with water?

• Is there an opportunity to see the situation differently?

• Explore the "inner story" from which you are meeting this reality. Can you modify your story?

Grounding Practices

Practice 8

• Create standing mountain pose.
• Place feet parallel and hips-width apart.
• Lift your toes and tone the muscles of your legs.
• Isometrically hug the midline with your legs.
• Bring the head of your arm bones up and towards your back, letting the bottom tip of your shoulder blades come together and rest. This will open your chest.
• Take your jawline back so that your face and heart are equally balanced.
• Draw your ribs in.
• Slowly lift and lower your arms with the rhythm of your breath. As your arms are moving, keep drawing the arms into the shoulder socket.
• Practice holding all of the above actions simultaneously and notice how you feel.

• Try to be gentle with your actions, but do hold all of the actions as you explore this level of integrated movement. Do you feel more grounded? More centered? Stronger? More alive?

There is also an energetic centering and grounding that accompanies the mental and physical practices. This can be most easily experienced by simple breath exercises:

Practice 9
• Diaphragmatic or belly breathing. This practice can be done seated or standing and can be added to any of the above practices as a way of becoming both centered and grounded.
• Bring one of your hands just below the navel on your belly.
• As you inhale, bring the breath down to the belly and push your hand out with your breath first. Continue to inhale up into the chest to your capacity.
• As you exhale, empty the breath from the lower belly first until empty of breath.

• Repeat breathing with both the inhale and the exhale commencing from the lower part of your belly just below the navel.

• You can release your hand from the belly once you understand how to physically bring the breath to the lower belly.

• As you inhale, visualize the energy moving down to the pelvic floor and to your feet.

• As you exhale, visualize the energy gently rising to the crown of your head and beyond.

Diaphragmatic breathing is the most efficient way of calming our nervous system. It grounds and relaxes us in the most primal way. If one is prone to anxiety this practice can be difficult at first. If one is used to being anxious or tense as a normal default state, as the body begins to relax it can cause a false sense of feeling out of control. My suggestion is to do the practice in short increments becoming acquainted with feeling relaxed. Once you break through the initial reaction it will be a wonderful tool.

Purification Practices

Practice 10

• Food Cleanse - For three days try a diet that consists of just "live foods" - Fruits, vegetables, salads, nuts - no animal products including dairy. Eliminate or greatly diminish caffeinated drinks.

• Speech Fast- For three days practice holding silence throughout your day (eat in silence, go inward, request from household members a morning/evening of silence. It does not have to be three days of total silence, just work on creating pockets of silence.

• Input Cleanse- For three days eliminate electronic input other than necessary for work. No TV, No Radio (in car also), No Social Platforms like FB, Twitter, etc.

• Spend time in nature. Take silent walks in the woods, at the beach. Open all of your senses and feel the harmony inherent in the natural world.

• Use these exercises as tools for becoming aware of the relationship we have to all of these "habits". Try not to judge but choose to be aware of how they are impacting your life. Start implementing these healthier life choices into your daily life. It is helpful not to focus on what you are giving up but instead look at what your are adding.

• Have a positive attitude about bringing life affirming changes into your daily experience.

• Expand these practices to a five day cycle.

Reframing the Minds Overlay

Practice 11

• Take a comfortable seat and commit to holding stillness.

• Close your eyes and begin to feel your body seated.

• Start to feel the breath as it pulses within you.

• Invite/cultivate a relaxed state within you. Release the jaw, relax the muscles of your face.

• Take a moment to recognize those individuals in your life who seem to tire you out and pull energy from you. It is their sense of lack, translated into need that places undue stress in your interactions with them.

• Now, scan your mind for people or situations where you may be feeling needy, scared and somehow wanting to control the situation, not to "upset the apple cart."

• Take a few minutes in meditation/contemplation to feel how your subconscious beliefs and fears might be impacting your emotions and behavior. Question/ challenge your own thoughts and beliefs. Separate the facts from your interpretations. (An example I use in my teachings is that when we are all sitting in the meditation room it is a "fact" -- we are all sitting in a room. Some may see it as a small or large room, a beautiful room, etc. These are the interpretations we place on reality. We can all agree to the fact that we are sitting in a room).

• Create a mental story where you can see yourself with love and peace stepping away from that situation/relationship knowing that all will be fine. Use affirmations - I am safe, I am loved, I am abundant…. to create the feeling state that those qualities belong to you and are not dependent on anyone else.

• Having created an internal vision of your own security and worthiness you can then reframe how you can interact in that situation from an energy neutral position. No one is needy. Your interactions come from generosity and a desire to give and share. You are letting go of the need to control the outcome allowing for its highest expression.

Practice 12

- Take a comfortable seat and commit to holding stillness.
- Close your eyes and begin to feel your body seated.
- Start to feel the breath as it pulses within you.
- Invite/cultivate a relaxed state within you - Release the jaw, relax the muscles of your face.
- Identify an aspect of yourself that is limiting you and that you would like to change.
- Identify its opposite, the quality that you would like to cultivate in yourself.
- Identify in which situations you already can feel this quality and deeply explore it while in this contemplative space. Really taste it and get intimate with it.
- Imagine/project the way you feel into other situations where in the past that has not been the case and see yourself embodying this quality you are cultivating.
- After having created this state within yourself, you are in a good place to try it out in real life. Take small steps in real life in the direction you want to develop in yourself.
- Focus on the quality you are developing in yourself and not on what has been challenging you.

ABOUT THE AUTHOR

Manuel Jose Muros (Manny) is a student of life, an author, a transformational consultant & mentor, and an avid spiritual teacher. Born in La Habana, Cuba, he had a spiritual awakening in his mid-thirties, which completely transformed his life.

As a Transformational Consultant & Mentor, he works with individuals and groups, teaching his unique Mind-Overlay curriculum, for becoming conscious and aware creators of our lives. He leads workshops and retreats in the US and internationally.

Manny is the founder of The Alnoba Peace Foundation, his New England home base for his teachings. An entrepreneur his entire professional life, Manny founded and served as president of two corporations. He was also the founder and vice chairman of the board of the first public Montessori Charter School in Massachusetts. For 17 years was the owner & Spiritual Director of the Yoga

Center of Newburyport. He holds a BS in Pharmacology and an MBA.

Manny's first book, "The Other Side Of Me - A Journey into the Mystical and the Gems Revealed", explores the mysteries behind the veil of life, explaining metaphysical/yogic teachings in a way that can be easily understood.

FOR MORE INFORMATION

For more information about attending events with
Manny, as well as to see blogs and videos,
please visit: www.manueljosemuros.com.

Made in the USA
Middletown, DE
27 January 2021

32575557R00052